MODERN MEN'S KNITS

JEN GEIGLEY

Welcome to Modern Men's Knits, a timeless collection of garments for men that are casual, contemporary and wearable. This collection brings modern shapes, a sophisticated colour palette and subtle details together to create a group of sweaters and accessories perfect for the modern man. I'm a minimalist at heart and I truly believe less is more and simple equals wearable. There's no greater satisfaction than finishing a hand-knit piece, trying it on and falling in love with it. Whether you're knitting a sweater for someone else or for yourself, the goal is to make go-to pieces that feel just right. I've included a sizing worksheet (pg 60) to make this process easier, especially if you're knitting a sweater for someone else. This worksheet will give you a space to record actual measurements, as well as measurements from an existing well-fitting sweater from your wardrobe, or from the wardrobe of the person you are knitting for. Whether your goal is a garment that is fitted or relaxed, this collection includes endless options to enhance your cosy, comfortable hand-knit wardrobe.

Photography • Quail Studio
Art Direction & Styling • Georgina Brant
Design Layout • Quail Studio
Model • Jack Green

First published in Great Britain in 2020 by
Quail Publishing Limited
Unit 15, Green Farm, Fritwell, Bicester, Oxfordshire, OX27 7QU
E-mail: info@quailstudio.co.uk

Modern Mens Knits
ISBN: 978-1-9162445-4-2

COLLECTION

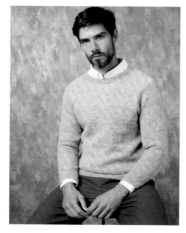

HORAN CREW NECK
pattern page 30

HORAN V NECK
pattern page 30

MERRICK
pattern page 34

COLDBROOK CREW NECK
pattern page 36

COLDBROOK V NECK
pattern page 36

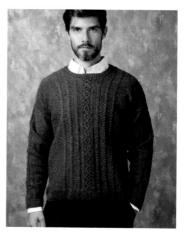

STILMAN
pattern page 42

BEACHMONT
pattern page 45

FAIRDALE
pattern page 47

CARBON
pattern page 49

RIVET
pattern page 50

CAMERON
pattern page 51

BEDFORD
pattern page 52

COSLEY
pattern page 39

HORAN

pattern page 30

—

MERRICK

pattern page 34

—

COLDBROOK

pattern page 36

—

COSLEY

pattern page 39

—

STILMAN

pattern page 42

—

BEACHMONT

pattern page 45

—

FAIRDALE

pattern page 47

—

CARBON

pattern page 49

—

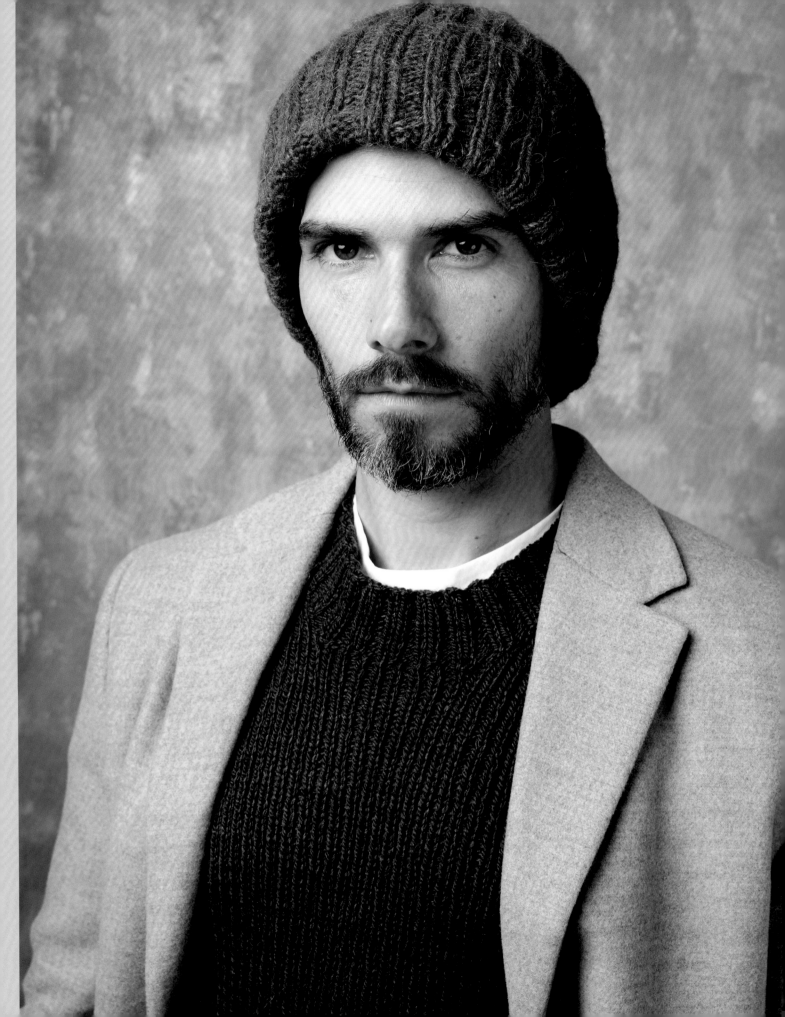

RIVET

pattern page 50

—

CAMERON

pattern page 51

—

BEDFORD

pattern page 52

—

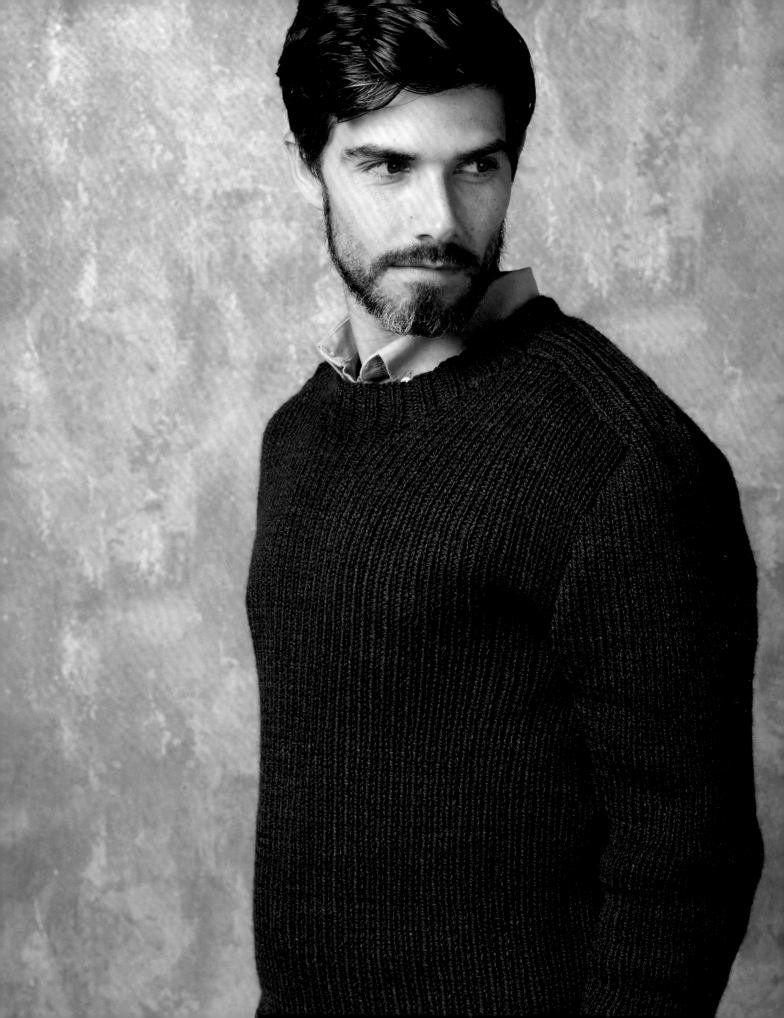

PATTERNS
—

HORAN

—

SIZE

	S	M	L	XL	XXL	XXXL	cm
To fit chest							
	102	107	112	117	122	127	cm
	40	42	44	46	48	50	in
Actual chest measurement of garment							
	111	118	124	129	136	142	cm
	44	46	49	51	54	56	in

YARN

Rowan Valley Tweed
Crew Neck – Malham 101

7	7	8	8	9	10	x 50gm

V-Neck – Curlew 119

7	7	8	8	9	10	x 50gm

NEEDLES

Size 3.25mm (no 10) (US 3) circular needles, 40 cm / 16 in and 80 cm / 32 in cm long
Set of 5, 3.25mm (no 10) (US 3) double-pointed needles

EXTRAS

Stitch markers
Stitch holders or scrap yarn

TENSION

24 sts and 36 rows to 10cm / 4in measured over st st, using 3.25mm (US 3) needles.

SPECIAL ABBREVIATIONS

M1L (Make 1 left): Insert left-hand needle from front to back under the strand between last st worked and next st on left-hand needle. Knit into the back loop to twist the stitch—one stitch increased.

M1R (Make 1 right): Insert left-hand needle from back to front under the strand between last st worked and next st on left-hand needle. Knit into the front loop to twist the stitch—one stitch increased.

NOTES

- Pullover is worked in one piece, from neck edge down
- When yoke is complete, body is joined in one piece and worked in rnds. Sleeves are worked in rnds on double-pointed needles.

PULLOVER WITH CREW NECK

YOKE

Using longer size 3.25mm (US 3) circular needle, loosely cast on 62 [62: 66: 70: 70: 70] sts.

Raglan Setup row (WS): P1, place marker (PM), P2 for left front raglan, PM, P6 [6: 6: 8: 8: 8] sts, PM, P2 for left back raglan, PM, P40 [40: 44: 44: 44: 44] sts, PM, P2 right back raglan, PM, P6 [6: 6: 8: 8: 8] sts, PM, P2 for right front raglan, PM, P1.

Row 1 (RS): Kfb, M1L, slip marker (SM), K2, SM, M1R, K to next marker, M1L, SM, K2, SM, M1R, K to next marker, M1L, SM, K2, SM, M1R, K to next marker, M1L, SM, K2, SM, M1R, Kfb. (10 sts inc). 72 [72: 76: 80: 80: 80] sts.

Row 2 and alt rows: Purl.

Row 3: K1, M1R, K to marker, M1L, SM, K2, SM, M1R, K to next marker, M1L, SM, k2, SM, M1R, K to next marker, M1L, SM, K2, SM, M1R, K to next marker, M1L, SM, K2, SM, M1R, K to last st, M1L, K1. (10 sts inc). 82 [82: 86: 90: 90: 90] sts.

Rep last 2 rows 9 times more, ending with a RS row. 172 [172: 176: 180: 180: 180] sts. Turn work and cast on 16 [16: 18: 18: 20: 20] sts for center front. With RS facing, join to beg working in rounds. PM for beg of rnd. 188 [188: 194: 198: 200: 200] sts.

Proceed in rounds as follows:

Round 1: Knit.

Round 2: K to marker, *M1L, SM, K2, SM, M1R**, K to next marker, rep from * twice more, then from * to ** once, K to end of round (8 sts inc). 196 [196: 202: 206: 208: 208] sts.

Round 3: Knit.

Rep last 2 rounds 30 [33: 34: 32: 32: 35] times more. 436 [460: 474: 462: 464: 488] sts.

Size 102 Only:
Knit 2 rounds.

Sizes 112 [117: 122: 127] Only:
Next round: K to marker, *M1L, SM, K2, SM, M1R**, K to next marker, rep from * twice more, then from * to ** once, K to end of round (8 sts inc). 482 [470: 472: 496] sts.
Next round: *K to marker, M1L, SM, K2, SM, K to next marker, SM, K2, SM, M1R, rep from * once more, K to end (4 sts inc). 486 [474: 476: 500] sts.
Rep last 2 rounds – [2: 4: 4] times more. 486 [498: 524: 548] sts.

All Sizes:
Divide for Sleeves and Body:
Next round: K to first marker, remove marker, k1. Slip next 92 [98: 102: 104: 108: 114] sts onto scrap yarn for left sleeve, removing the 2 markers. Cast on 6 [6: 6: 8: 8: 8] sts for underarm, placing marker after 3rd [3rd: 3rd: 4th: 4th: 4th] st for beg of round. K next 126 [132: 141: 145: 154: 160] sts for back, removing the 2 markers. Slip next 92 [98: 102: 104: 108: 114] sts onto scrap yarn for right sleeve, removing the 2 markers. Cast on 6 [6: 6: 8: 8: 8] sts for underarm. K last 126 [132: 141: 145: 154: 160] sts for front, removing the raglan marker and original beg of rnd marker. 264 [276: 294: 306: 324: 336] sts for body.

BODY
Knit even in rounds on these 264 [276: 294: 306: 324: 336] sts until body from underarm meas 42 [42: 43: 44.5: 47: 47] cm.
Next round: *K1, P1, rep from * around.
Last round forms rib.
Rep last round until rib meas 6.5cm.
Cast off loosely in rib.

SLEEVES
Slip 92 [98: 102: 104: 108: 114] sts from scrap yarn onto size 3.25mm (US 3) double-pointed needles, rejoin yarn and knit across. Pick up and K6 [6: 6: 8: 8: 8] sts along underarm, placing marker after 3rd [3rd: 3rd: 4th: 4th: 4th] st for beg of round. Divide sts evenly between 4 needles and join in round. 98 [104: 108: 112: 116: 122] sts.
Knit 3 rounds.
Next (dec) round: K1, k2tog, knit to last 3 sts, skp, k1. 96 [102: 106: 110: 114: 120] sts.
Rep dec round every foll 4th round to 54 [60: 58: 60: 68: 66] sts, then every foll 6th round until there are 50 [54: 56: 58: 62: 64] sts.
Knit even in rounds until sleeve from underarm meas 40.5 [41: 41: 43: 44: 46] cm.

Cuff
Next round: *K1, P1, rep from * around.
Last round forms rib.
Rep last round until rib meas 6.5cm.
Cast off loosely in rib.

MAKING UP
Press as described on the information page.

COLLAR
With RS facing, using shorter size 3.25mm (US 3) circular needle and starting at left back raglan, pick up and K108 [108: 114: 118: 120: 120] sts evenly around neck opening. PM and join to beg working in rounds.
Next round: *K1, P1, rep from * around.
Last round forms rib.
Rep last round 9 times more.
Cast off loosely in rib.

PULLOVER WITH V-NECK
YOKE
Using longer size 3.25mm (US 3) circular needle, loosely cast on 62 [62: 66: 70: 70: 70] sts.
Raglan Setup row (WS): P1, place marker (PM), P2 for left front raglan, PM, P6 [6: 6: 8: 8: 8] sts, PM, P2 for left back raglan, PM, P40 [40: 44: 44: 44: 44] sts, PM, P2 right back raglan, PM, P6 [6: 6: 8: 8: 8] sts, PM, P2 for right front raglan, PM, P1.
Row 1 (RS): K1, M1L, slip marker (SM), K2, SM, M1R, K to next marker, M1L, SM, K2, SM, M1R, K to next marker, M1L, SM, K2, SM, M1R, K to next marker, M1L, SM, K2, SM, M1R, K1 (8 sts inc). 70 [70: 74: 78: 78: 78] sts.
Row 2: Purl.
Row 3: K1, M1R, K to marker, M1L, SM, K2, SM, M1R, K to next marker, M1L, SM, k2, SM, M1R, K to next marker, M1L, SM, K2, SM, M1R, K to next marker, M1L, SM, K2, SM, M1R, K to last st, M1L, K1. (10 sts inc). 80 [80: 84: 88: 88: 88] sts.
Row 4: Purl.
Row 5: K to marker, M1L, SM, K2, SM, M1R, K to next marker, M1L, SM, K2, SM, M1R, K to next marker, M1L, SM, K2, SM, M1R, K to next marker, M1L, SM, K2, SM, M1R, K to end. (8 sts inc). 88 [88: 92: 96: 96: 96] sts.
Row 6: Purl.
Rep last 4 rows 18 [18: 19: 19: 20: 20] times more. 412 [412: 434: 438: 456: 456] sts.
Next row (RS): K to marker, M1L, SM, K2, SM, M1R, K to next marker, M1L, SM, K2, SM, M1R, K to next marker, M1L, SM, K2, SM, M1R, K to end. (8 sts inc). With RS facing, join fronts to beg working in rounds. PM at center front for beg of rnd. 420 [420: 442: 446: 464: 464] sts
Proceed in rounds as follows:
Round 1: Knit.

Sizes S [M: L: XL and XXXL] Only:
Round 2: K to marker, *M1L, SM, K2, SM, M1R**, K to next marker, rep from * twice more, then from * to ** once, K to end of round (8 sts inc). 428 [428: 450: 454: 472] sts.
Round 3: Knit.
Rep last 2 rounds 1 [4: 3: 1: 2] times more. 436 [460: 474: 462: 488] sts.

Size 102 Only:
Knit 2 rounds.

Sizes L [XL: XXL: XXXL] Only:
Next round: K to marker, *M1L, SM, K2, SM, M1R**, K to next marker, rep from * twice more, then from * to ** once, K to end of round (8 sts inc). 482 [470: 472: 496] sts.
Next round: *K to marker, M1L, SM, K2, SM, K to next marker, SM, K2, SM, M1R, rep from * once more, K to end (4 sts inc). 486 [474: 476: 500] sts.
Rep last 2 rounds – [2: 4: 4] times more. 486 [498: 524: 548] sts.

All Sizes:
Divide for Sleeves and Body:
Next round: K to first marker, remove marker, k1. Slip next 92 [98: 102: 104: 108: 114] sts onto scrap yarn for left sleeve, removing the 2 markers. Cast on 6 [6: 6: 8: 8: 8] sts for underarm, placing marker after 3rd [3rd: 3rd: 4th: 4th: 4th] st for beg of round. K next 126 [132: 141: 145: 154: 160] sts for back, removing the 2 markers. Slip next 92 [98: 102: 104: 108: 114] sts onto scrap yarn for right sleeve, removing the 2 markers. Cast on 6 [6: 6: 8: 8: 8] sts for underarm. K last 126 [132: 141: 145: 154: 160] sts for front, removing the raglan marker and original beg of rnd marker. 264 [276: 294: 306: 324: 336] sts for body.

BODY
Work as given for body of Pullover with Crew Neck.

SLEEVES
Work as given for sleeves of Pullover with Crew Neck.

MAKING UP
Press as described on the information page.

NECKBAND
With RS facing, using shorter 3.25mm (US 3) circular needle and starting at centre front, pick up and K 56 [56: 58: 58: 60: 60] sts evenly along right front neck edge, pick up and K 61 [61: 65: 69: 69: 69] sts along cast-on edge, pick up and K 56 [56: 58: 58: 60: 60] sts evenly along left front neck edge to center front. 173 [173: 181: 185: 189: 189] sts.
Do not join, work back and forth in rows.
Row 1 (WS): *P1, K1, rep from * to last st, P1.
Row 2: K1, *P1, K1, rep from * to end.
Last 2 rows form rib.
Rep last 2 rows 4 times more.
Cast off loosely in rib.
Overlapping left front neck edging over right, neatly sew edges of neck edging along pick-up row.

Crew neck

V neck

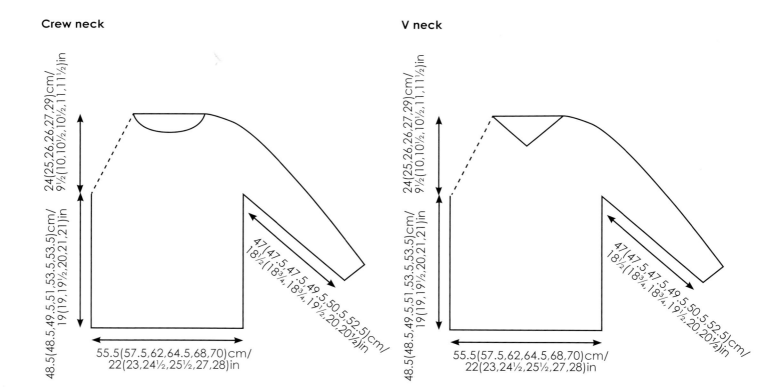

24(25,26,26,27,29)cm/
9½(10,10½,10½,11,11½)in

48.5(48.5,49.5,51,53.5,53.5)cm/
19(19,19½,20,21,21)in

47(47.5,47.5,49,50.5,52.5)cm/
18½(18¾,18¾,19½,20,20½)in

55.5(57.5,62,64.5,68,70)cm/
22(23,24½,25½,27,28)in

MERRICK

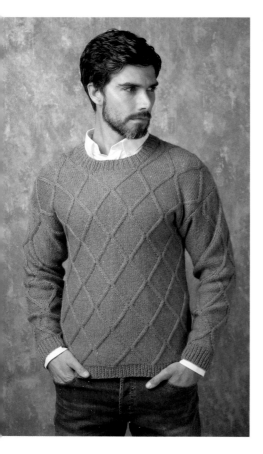

SIZE

	S	M	L	XL	XXL	XXXL	cm
To fit chest							
	102	107	112	117	122	127	cm
	40	42	44	46	48	50	in
Actual chest measurement of garment							
	110.5	116	120.5	128	130.5	135	cm
	43½	45½	47½	50½	51½	53	in

YARN

Rowan Moordale

	6	6	7	7	8	8	x 100gm

(photographed in Turmeric)

NEEDLES

4mm (no 8) (US 6) needles
4mm (no 8) (US 6) circular needle, 40 cm / 16 in long
Cable needle
Stitch holders

TENSION

21 sts and 32 rows to 10 cm / 4 in over Diamond
pattern using 4mm (US 6) needles.

STITCHES

Cable 3 Right (C3R): Slip next stitch onto cable needle,
hold at back of work, K2 from left-hand needle, P 1 st
from cable needle.
Cable 3 Left (C3L): Slip the next two stitches onto
cable needle, hold a front of work, P1 from left-hand
needle, K 2 sts from cable needle.

DIAMOND PATTERN - worked over 22 sts

Row 1 (RS): P8, C3R, C3L, P8; rep from * to end.
Row 2 and every alt row: Work each st as it presents.
Row 3: P7, C3R, P2, C3L, P7; rep from * to end.
Row 5: P6, C3R, P4, C3L, P6; rep from * to end.
Row 7: P5, C3R, P6, C3L, P5; rep from * to end.
Row 9: P4, C3R, P8, C3L, P4; rep from * to end.
Row 11: P3, C3R, P10, C3L, P3; rep from * to end.
Row 13: P2, C3R, P12, C3L, P2; rep from * to end.
Row 15: P1, C3R, P14, C3L, P1; rep from * to end.
Row 17: C3R, P16, C3L; rep from * to end.
Row 19: C3L, P16, C3R; rep from * to end.
Row 21: P1, C3R, P14, C3L, P1; rep from * to end.
Row 23: P2, C3R, P12, C3L, P2; rep from * to end.
Row 25: P3, C3R, P10, C3L, P3; rep from * to end.
Row 27: P4, C3R, P8, C3L, P4; rep from * to end.

Row 29: P5, C3R, P6, C3L, P5; rep from * to end.
Row 31: P6, C3R, P4, C3L, P6; rep from * to end.
Row 33: P7, C3R, P2, C3L, P7; rep from * to end.
Row 35: P8, C3R, C3L, P8; rep from * to end.
Row 36: Work each st as it presents.
Rep rows 1 to 36 for diamond pattern.

BACK

Using 4mm (US 6) needles, cast on 116 (122: 126: 134:
138: 142) sts.
Row 1 (RS): * K1, P1, rep from * to end.
Last row sets rib.
Work in rib pattern for a further 11 rows.
Row 1 (RS): P3 (6: 8: 1: 3: 5), work row 1 of diamond
pattern 5 (5: 5: 6: 6: 6) times, P3 (6: 8: 1: 3: 5).
Row 2: K3 (6: 8: 1: 3 5), work row 2 of diamond pattern
5 (5: 5: 6: 6: 6) times, K3 (6: 8: 1: 3: 5).
Last 2 rows set diamond pattern with edge stitches.
Work in diamond pattern working chart rows 1 – 36
and edge stitches throughout until back measures
68 (69: 70: 71: 72: 73) cm, ending with a WS row.

Shape shoulders

Cast off 21 (22: 23: 24: 25: 26) sts at beg of next 4 rows.
32 [34: 34: 38: 38: 38] sts.
Leave rem sts on a stitch holder or scrap yarn for
back neck.

FRONT

Work as for back until 26 (30: 30: 38: 38: 38) rows less have been worked to start of shoulder shaping, ending with a WS row.

Shape neck

Keeping cable pattern correct throughout, continue as folls:

Next Row (RS): Patt 48 (51: 53: 57: 59: 61), turn. Leave rem sts unworked.

Next Row: Patt to end.

Next Row: Patt to last 2 sts, patt 2tog. 47 [50: 52: 56: 58: 60] sts.

Work in pattern for 3 rows.

Rep last 4 rows until 42 (44: 46: 48: 50: 52) sts remain.

Cont straight until front is the same length as back to start of shoulder shaping, ending with a WS row.

Shape shoulders

Cast off 21 (22: 23: 24: 25: 26) sts at beg of next and foll alt row.

Fasten off.

With RS facing slip next 20 sts onto a stitch holder.

Rejoin yarn to rem 48 (51: 53: 57: 59: 61) sts and patt to end.

Work as for other side of neck, reversing shapings.

SLEEVES

Using 4mm (US 6) needles, cast on 58 (58: 64: 64: 68: 68) sts.

Row 1 (RS): * K1, P1, rep from * to end.

Last row sets rib.

Work in rib pattern for a further 11 rows.

Next Row (RS): P7 (7: 10: 10: 1: 1), work row 1 of diamond pattern 2 (2: 2: 2: 3: 3) times, P7 (7: 10: 10: 1: 1).

Next Row: K7 (7: 10: 10: 1: 1), work row 2 of diamond pattern 2 (2: 2: 2: 3: 3) times, K7 (7: 10: 10: 1: 1).

Last 2 rows set diamond pattern with edge stitches.

Work in diamond pattern working chart rows 1 – 36 with edge stitches throughout, AND AT SAME TIME, inc 1 st at each end of

8th row to 92 (96: 100: 106: 110: 110) sts.

Cont without shaping until sleeve measures 53 (55: 55: 58: 58: 60) cm, ending with a WS row.

Cast off loosely in pattern.

MAKING UP

Press as described on the information page.

Join both shoulder seams using mattress stitch.

Neckband

Using 4mm (US 6) circular needle, pick up and knit 22 (24: 24: 30: 30: 30) sts down left front neck, knit 20 sts from front neck stitch holder, pick up and knit 22 (24: 24: 30: 30: 30) sts up right front neck, knit 32 (34: 34: 38: 38: 38) sts from back neck stitch holder. 96 [102: 102: 118: 118: 118] sts. Join to work in round, placing marker at beg of rnd.

Next Rnd: *K1, P1, rep from * to end.

Rep last round for a further 9 rounds.

Cast off loosely.

Place markers 22 (23: 24: 25: 26: 26) cm down from shoulders on front and back. Sew top of sleeve between markers.

Join side and sleeve seams.

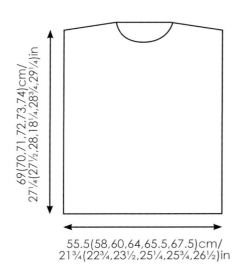

55.5(58,60,64,65.5,67.5)cm/
21¾(22¾,23½,25¼,25¾,26½)in

69(70,71,72,73,74)cm/
27¼(27½,28,18¼,28¾,29¼)in

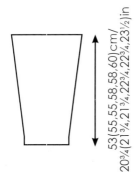

53(55,55,58,58,60)cm/
20¾(21¾,21¾,22¾,22¾,23½)in

COLDBROOK

SIZE

	S	M	L	XL	XXL	XXXL	
To fit chest							cm
	102	107	112	117	122	127	cm
	40	42	44	46	48	50	in
Actual chest measurement of garment							
	113	118	124	128	133	138	cm
	44½	46½	48¾	50½	52¼	54¼	in

YARN
Rowan Softyak DK
V neck - Submarine 00251

	S	M	L	XL	XXL	XXXL	
	10	11	12	13	14	15	x 50gm

Crew neck – Plauteau

	S	M	L	XL	XXL	XXXL	
	11	12	13	14	15	16	x 50gm

NEEDLES
4mm (no 8) (US 6) needles
Set of four 4mm (no 8) (US 6) double-pointed needles (dpn's)
4mm (no 8) (US 6) circular needle, 40 cm / 16 in long

EXTRAS
Stitch holders
Stitch markers

TENSION
22 sts and 30 rows to 10 cm / 4 in measured over st st using 4mm (US 6) needles.

BACK – both versions
Using 4mm (US 6) needles, cast on 124 (130: 136: 140: 146: 152) sts.
Next Row (RS): *K1, P1, rep from * to end.
Last row sets rib pattern.
Work in rib pattern for a further 9 rows.

Starting with a K row, work in st st as folls:

Optional Lower Back Short Rows (to add length to back of sweater)
Work in st st until back measures approximately 15 cm / 6 in, ending with a WS row.
Work short rows as folls:
Row 1 (RS): Knit to last 5 sts, wrap and turn.
Row 2: Purl to last 5 sts, wrap and turn.
Row 3 (RS): Knit to last 8 sts, wrap and turn.
Row 4: Purl to last 8 sts, wrap and turn.
Row 5 (RS): Knit to last 10 sts, wrap and turn.
Row 6: Purl to last 10 sts, wrap and turn.

Next row (RS): Knit to end of row, picking up loops from wrap stitches.
Cont in st st until back measures 66 (67: 68: 68: 69: 69) cm, ending with a WS row.

Shape shoulders
Cast off 20 (21: 22: 23: 24: 26) sts at beg of next 4 (4: 2: 2: 2: 4) rows, then 0 (0: 23: 24: 25: 0) sts on foll 2 rows.
44 [46: 46: 46: 48: 48] sts.
Leave rem sts on a stitch holder for back neck.

FRONT – V-neck version
Work as for back (omitting optional lower back short rows) until front measures 49 (50: 50: 50: 50: 50) cm, ending with a WS row.

Shape front neck
Next Row (RS): Knit 58 (61: 64: 66: 69: 72) sts, Sl 1, K1, psso, K2, turn. Leave rem sts unworked.
61 [64: 67: 69: 72: 75] sts.
Next Row: Purl
Next Row: K to last 4 sts, Sl 1, K1, psso, K2. 60 [63: 66: 68: 71: 74] sts.
Rep last 2 rows until 40 (42: 45: 47: 49: 52) sts remain, ending with a RS row.
Cont straight until front is the same length of back to shoulder shaping, ending with a WS row.

Shape shoulders

Cast off 20 (21: 22: 23: 24: 26) sts at beg of next 2 (2: 1: 1: 1: 2) alt rows, then 0 (0: 23: 24: 25: 0) sts on foll alt row.
Fasten off.
With RS facing, rejoin yarn to rem 62 (65: 68: 70: 73: 76) sts, K2, K2tog, K to end. 61 [64: 67: 69: 72: 75] sts.
Work as for other side of neck, reversing shapings.

FRONT – crew neck version

Work as for back (omitting optional lower back short rows) until front measures 57 (58: 59: 59: 60: 60) cm, ending with a WS row.

Shape front neck.

Next Row (RS): K57 (60: 63: 65: 68: 71) sts, turn. Leave rem sts unworked.
Next Row: P2, P2tog tbl, P to end. 56 [59: 62: 64: 67: 70] sts.
Next Row: K to last 4 sts, Sl 1, K1, psso, K2. 55 [58: 61: 63: 66: 69] sts.
Rep last 2 rows to 40 (42: 45: 47: 49: 52) sts.
Cont straight until front is the same length as back to start of shoulder shaping, ending with a WS row.

Shape shoulders

Cast off 20 (21: 22: 23: 24: 26) sts at beg of next 2 (2: 1: 1: 1: 2) alt rows, then 0 (0: 23: 24: 25: 0) sts on foll alt row.
Fasten off.
With RS facing, slip next 10 sts onto a stitch holder.
Rejoin yarn to rem 57 (60: 63: 65: 68: 71) sts and knit to end of row.
Work as for other side of neck, reversing shapings.
Fasten off.

SLEEVES – both versions

Using 4mm (US 6) dpn's, cast on 56 (60: 62: 66: 68: 70) sts.
Divide sts evenly over 3 needles. Join to work in round being careful not to twist sts, and placing marker for beg of rnd.
Next Rnd: *K1, P1, rep from * to end.
Last rounds sets rib.
Work in rib for a further 8 rounds.
Knit 4 rnds.
Next (inc) rnd: K1, M1R, K to last st, M1L, K1. 58 [62: 64: 68: 70: 72] sts.
Working in st st throughout (knit every rnd), inc 2 sts as set above on every foll 10th (10th: 10th: 10th: 10th: 8th) round to 84 (88: 92: 96: 102: 106) sts.
Cont without shaping until sleeve measures 52 (54: 56: 58: 60: 62) cm, from cast on edge.
Cast off.

MAKING UP

Press as described on the information page.
Join both shoulder seams using mattress stitch.

Neckbands
V neck version

Using 4mm (US 6) circular needle, pick up and knit 46 (46: 48: 48: 50: 50) sts down left front neck, place marker, pick up 1 st at base of V, place marker, pick up and knit 46 (46: 48: 48: 50: 50) sts up right front neck, knit 44 (46: 46: 46: 48: 48) sts from back neck stitch holder. 137 [139: 143: 143: 149: 149] sts. Join to work in round, placing marker at beg of rnd.
Next Rnd: *K1, P1, rep from * to end.
Next Rnd: Patt to 2 sts before marker, K2tog, slip marker, K1, slip marker, Sl 1, K1, psso, patt to end. 135 [137: 141: 141: 147: 147] sts.
Next Rnd: Patt to end.
Rep last 2 rounds 3 times more. 129 [131: 135: 135: 141: 141] sts.
Cast off loosely.

Crew neck version

Using 4mm (US 6) circular needle, pick up and knit 24 (25: 26: 27: 28: 29) sts down left front neck, knit 10 sts from front neck stitch holder, pick up and knit 24 (25: 26: 27: 28: 29) sts up right front neck, knit 44 (46: 46: 46: 48: 48) sts from back neck stitch holder. 102 [106: 108: 110: 114: 116] sts. Join to work in round, placing marker at beg of rnd.
Nexr Rnd: *K1, P1, rep from * to end.
Last rnd sets rib.
Work in rib for a further 9 rnds.
Cast off loosely.

Place markers 19 (20: 21: 22: 23.5: 24) cm down from shoulders on front and back. Sew top of sleeve between markers.
Join side and sleeve seams.

V neck

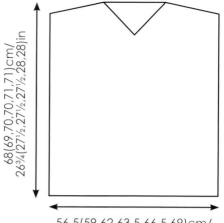

68(69,70,70,71,71)cm/
26¾(27½,27½,27½,28,28)in

56.5(59,62,63.5,66.5,69)cm/
22¼(23¼,24½,25,26¼,27¼)in

Crew neck

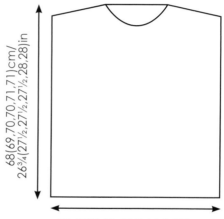

68(69,70,70,71,71)cm/
26¾(27½,27½,27½,28,28)in

56.5(59,62,63.5,66.5,69)cm/
22¼(23¼,24½,25,26¼,27¼)in

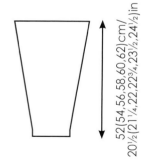

52(54,56,58,60,62)cm/
20½(21¼,22,22¾,23½,24½)in

COSLEY

SIZE

	S	M	L	XL	XXL	XXXL	cm
To fit chest							
	102	107	112	117	122	127	cm
	40	42	44	46	48	50	in
Actual chest measurement of garment							
	114	119	124	129	134	139	cm
	45	46½	48¾	50½	52½	54¾	in

YARN

Rowan Island Blend

	11	12	12	13	13	14	x 50gm

(photographed in Jet 902)

NEEDLES

4mm (no 8) (US 6) needles
4mm (no 8) (US 6) circular needle, 40 cm / 16 in long

EXTRAS

Stitch holders
Stitch markers

TENSION

21 sts and 28 rows to 10 cm / 4 in measured over rib using 4mm (US 6) needles **once blocked.**

BACK

Using 4mm (US 6) needles, cast on 118 (122: 130: 134: 138: 146) sts.
Row 1 (RS): K2, *P2, K2, rep from * to end.
Row 2: *P2, K2, rep from * to last 2 sts, P2.
Last 2 rows set rib pattern.
Work in rib pattern for a further 10 rows, increasing 1 (1: 0: 0: 1: 0) st at each end of last row. 120 [124: 130: 134: 140: 146] sts.
Next Row (RS): *K1, P1, rep from * to end.
Last row sets single rib pattern.
Cont in single rib patt as folls:

Optional Lower Back Short Rows (to add length to back of sweater)

Work in single rib patt until back measures approximately 15 cm / 6 in, ending with a WS row.
Keeping single rib patt correct, work short rows as folls:
Row 1 (RS): Work in rib to last 5 sts, wrap and turn.
Row 2: Work in rib to last 5 sts, wrap and turn.
Row 3 (RS): Work in rib to last 8 sts, wrap and turn.

Row 4: Work in rib to last 8 sts, wrap and turn.
Row 5 (RS): Work in rib to last 10 sts, wrap and turn.
Row 6: Work in rib to last 10 sts, wrap and turn.
Next row (RS): Work in rib to end of row, picking up loops from wrap stitches.
Cont in single rib pattern until back measures 40 (41: 42: 43: 44: 45) cm, ending with a WS row.

Shape Armholes

Cast off 6 sts at beg of next 2 rows. 108 [112: 118: 122: 128: 134] sts.
Dec 1 st at each end of next and foll alt row.
104 [108: 114: 118: 124: 130] sts.
Cont without shaping until armholes measure 24 (24: 25: 25: 25.5: 25.5)cm, ending with a WS row.

Shape Shoulders

Cast off 8 (8: 9: 9: 10: 10) sts at beg of next 8 (6: 6: 8: 4: 6) rows, then 0 (9: 8: 0: 9: 11) sts on foll 0 (2: 2: 0: 4: 2) rows. 40 [42: 44: 46: 48: 48] sts.
Leave rem sts on stitch holder for back neck.

FRONT

Work as for back (omitting optional lower back short rows) until 14 (16: 16: 16: 18: 18) rows less have been worked to start of shoulder shaping, ending with a WS row.

Shape front neck

Keeping rib patt correct throughout, continue as folls:

Next Row (RS): Patt 44 (46: 49: 50: 53: 56) sts, turn.
Leave rem sts unworked.

Next Row: Patt to end.

Dec 1 st at neck edge of next and every foll row until 32 (33: 35: 36: 38: 41) sts rem.

Work 0 (1: 0: 0: 1: 1) row, ending with a WS row.

Shape shoulders

Cast off 8 (8: 9: 9: 10: 10) sts at beg of next and foll alt 3 (2: 2: 3: 1: 2) rows, then 0 (9: 8: 0: 9: 11) sts at beg of foll 0 (1: 1: 0: 2: 1) alt rows.

Fasten off.

With RS facing slip next 16 (16: 16: 18: 18: 18) sts onto stitch holder for front neck. Rejoin yarn to rem 44 (46: 49: 50: 53: 56) sts and patt to end.

Work as for other side of neck, reversing shapings.

SLEEVES

Using 4mm (US 6) needles, cast on 54 (54: 58: 58: 62: 62) sts.

Row 1 (RS): K2, *P2, K2, rep from * to end.

Row 2: *P2, K2, rep from * to last 2 sts, P2.

Last 2 rows set rib pattern.

Work in rib pattern for a further 10 rows, increasing 1 (1: 0: 0: 1: 1) st at each end of last row.

56[56: 58: 58: 64: 64] sts.

Next Row (RS): *K1, P1, rep from * to end.

Last row sets single rib pattern.

Working in single rib patt throughout, inc 1 st at each end of next and every foll 6th row to 84 (84: 86: 86: 68: 68) sts, then every foll 4th row to 98 (98: 100: 100: 102: 102) sts, bringing increase sts into single rib patt.

Cont without shaping until sleeve measures 45 (46: 47: 48: 49: 49) cm, ending with a WS row.

Shape sleeve cap

Cast off 6 sts at beg of next 2 rows. 86 [86: 88: 88: 90: 90] sts.

Dec 1 st at each end of next and foll alt row to 18 sts, ending with a WS row.

Shoulder epaulet

Working on these 18 sts only, work in single rib patt as established until shoulder epaulet measures 15 (15.5: 16.5: 17: 18: 19) cm when slightly stretched, ending with a WS row.

Place sts on holder.

MAKING UP

Press as described on the information page, ensuring stitches match tension stated.

Join side edges of shoulder epaulets to front and back shoulders.

Neckband

Using 4mm (US 6) circular needle, knit 18 sts from left shoulder epaulet, pick up and knit 12 (13: 13: 13: 15 15) sts down left front neck, knit 16 (16: 16: 18: 18: 18) sts from front neck stitch holder, knit 18 sts from right shoulder epaulet, pick up and knit 12 (13: 13: 13: 15: 15) sts up right front neck, knit 40 (42: 44: 46: 48: 48) sts from back neck stitch holder decreasing 0 (0: 2: 2: 0: 0) sts across. 116 [120: 120: 124: 132: 132] sts. Join to work in round, placing marker at beg of rnd.

Next Rnd: *K2, P2, rep from * to end.

Rep last round for a further 11 rounds.

Cast off loosely in patt.

Sew in sleeves.

Join side and sleeve seams.

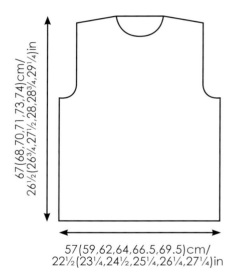

67(68,70,71,73,74)cm/
26½(26¾,27½,28,28¾,29¼)in

57(59,62,64,66.5,69.5)cm/
22½(23¼,24½,25¼,26¼,27¼)in

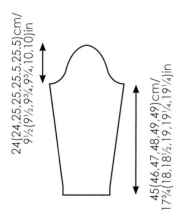

24(24,25,25.5,25.5,25.5)cm/
9½(9½,9¾,10,10,10)in

45(46,47,48,49,49)cm/
17¾(18,18½,19,19¼,19¼)in

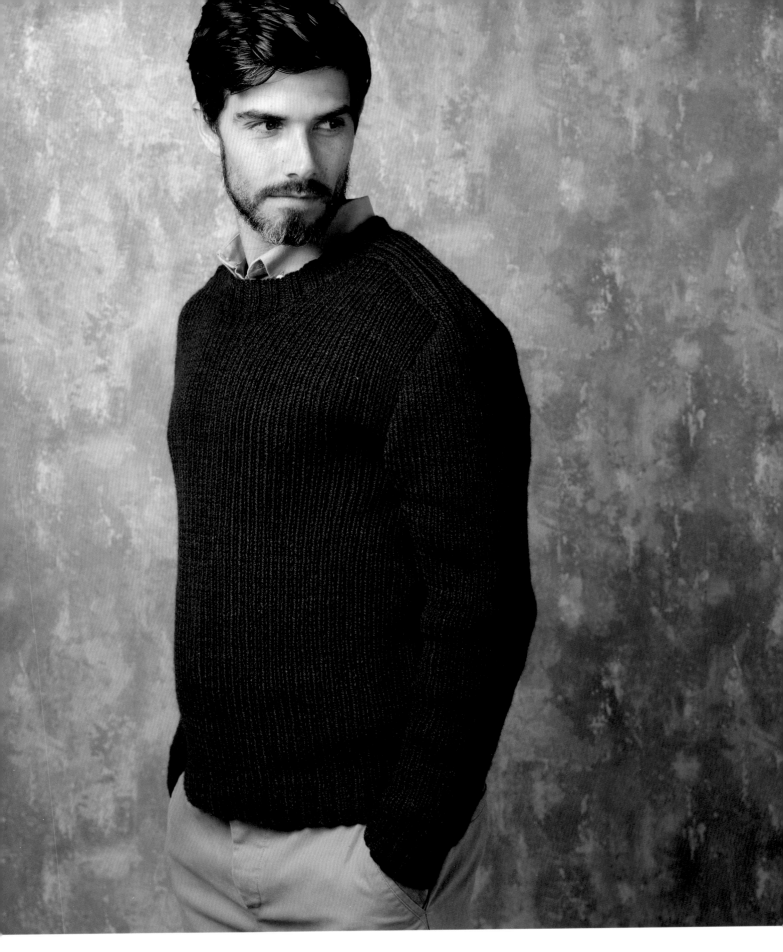

STILMAN

SIZE

	S	M	L	XL	XXL	XXXL	
To fit chest							
	102	107	112	117	122	127	cm
	40	42	44	46	48	50	in
Actual chest measurement of garment							
	107	112	117	122	127	132	cm
	42	44	46	48	50	52	in

YARN

Rowan Valley Tweed

	8	9	9	10	10	11	x 50gm

(photographed in Lapwing 114)

NEEDLES

3.25mm (no 10) (US 3) needles
3.25mm (no 10) (US 3) circular needle, 40 cm / 16 in long
Cable needle

EXTRAS

Stitch holders
Stitch markers

TENSION

24 sts and 36 rows to 10 cm / 4 in measured over rev st st using 3.25mm (US 3) needles.

STITCHES

Cable 4 Right (C4R): Slip the next 2 sts onto cable needle, hold at back of work, K2, P2 from cable needle.

Cable 4 Left (C4L): Slip the next 2 sts onto cable needle, hold a front of work, P2, K2 from cable needle.

Cross 4 Back (C4B): Slip the next 2 sts onto cable needle, hold at back of work, K2, K2 from cable needle.

Cross 4 Front (C4F): Slip the next 2 sts onto cable needle, hold a front of work, K2, K2 from cable needle.

Cross 6 Back (C6B): Slip the next 3 sts onto cable needle, hold at back of work, K3, K3 from cable needle.

Cross 6 Front (C6F): Slip the next 3 sts onto cable needle, hold a front of work, K3, K3 from cable needle.

Body Cable Pattern;

Row 1(RS): K4, P6, K6, P6, K4, P4, K2, P2, C4R, C4L, P2, K2, P4, K4, P6, K6, P6, K4.

Row 2 and all WS Rows: P4, K6, P6, K6, P4, K4, P2, work sts in manner they present, P2, K4, P4, K6, P6, K6, P4.

Row 3: C4B, P6, C6B, P6, C4B, P4, K2, C4R, P4, C4L, K2, P4, C4F, P6, C6B, P6, C4F.

Row 5: K4, P6, K6, P6, K4, P4, K2, P4, C4B, P4, K2, P4, K4, P6, K6, P6, K4.

Row 7: C4B, P6, K6, P6, C4B, P6, C4L, P4, C4R, P6, C4F, P6, K6, P6, C4F.

Row 9: K4, P6, C6B, P6, K4, P4, K2, P2, C4L, C4R, P2, K2, P4, K4, P6, C6F, P6, K4.

Row 11: C4B, P6, K6, P6, C4B, P4, K2, P4, C4F, P4, K2, P4, C4F, P6, K6, P6, C4F.

Row 12: P4, K6, P6, K6, P4, K4, P2, SL M work sts in manner they present to marker, SL M, P2, K4, P4, K6, P6, K6, P4.

Sleeve Cable Pattern;

Row 1 (RS): K4, P4, K2, P2, C4R, C4L, P2, K2, P4, K4.

Row 2 and all WS Rows: P4, K4, P2, work sts in manner they present to marker, K2, P4, K4.

Row 3: C4B, P4, K2, C4R, P4, C4L, K2, P4, C4F.

Row 5: K4, P4, K2, P4, C4B, P4, K2, P4, K4.

Row 7: C4B, P6, C4L, P4, C4R, P6, C4F.

Row 9: K4, P4, K2, P2, C4L, C4R, P2, K2, P4, K4.

Row 11: C4B, P4, K2, P4, C4F, P4, K2, P4, C4F.

Row 12: P4, K4, P2, work sts in manner they present, K2, P4, K4.

BACK
Using 3.25mm (US 3) needles, cast on 154 (160: 166: 172: 178: 184) sts.
Next Row (RS): * K1, P1, rep from * to end.
Last row sets rib pattern.
Work in rib for a further 13 rows.
Row 1 (RS): P39 (42: 45: 48: 51: 54) sts, work across 76 sts of row 1 of body cable pattern, P39 (42: 45: 48: 51: 54) sts.
Row 2: K39 (42: 45: 48: 51: 54) sts, work across 76 sts of row 2 of body cable pattern, K39 (42: 45: 48: 51: 54) sts.
Last 2 rows set cable pattern with rev st st on either side.
Work in pattern, repeating cable pattern rows 1 – 12, until back measures 66 (67: 68: 69: 70: 71) cm, ending with a WS row.

Shape shoulders
Cast off 15 (15: 16: 16: 17: 17) sts at beg of 8 [6: 8: 6: 8: 6] rows, then 0 (16: 0: 17: 0: 18) sts at beg of foll 2 rows.
34 [38: 38: 42: 42: 46] sts.
Leave rem sts on stitch holder for back neck.

FRONT
Work as for back until work measures 9 cm less than back to start of shoulder shaping, ending with a WS row.

Shape front neck
Next Row (RS): Patt 65 (68: 71: 74: 77: 80) sts, turn.
Leave rem sts unworked.
Next Row (WS): Patt to end.
Next Row: Patt to last 2 sts, K2tog. 64 [67: 70: 73: 76: 79] sts.
Next Row: Patt to end.
Cont working in patt, decreasing 1 st at neck edge on next and every alt row until 60 (61: 64: 65: 68: 69) sts remain, ending with a WS row.
Cont straight until front is the same length as back to start of shoulder shaping, ending with a WS row.

Shape shoulders
Cast off 15 (15: 16: 16: 17: 17) sts at beg of next and foll 3 [2: 3: 2: 3: 2] rows, then 0 (16: 0: 17: 0: 18] sts on foll alt row. Fasten off.
With RS facing, slip next 24 sts onto a stitch holder for front neck. Rejoin yarn to rem 65 (68: 71: 74: 77: 80) sts and patt to end.
Work as for other side of neck, reversing shapings.

SLEEVES
Using 3.25mm (US 3) needles, cast on 68 (68: 74: 74: 80: 80) sts.
Next Row (RS): * K1, P1, rep from * to end.
Last row sets rib pattern.
Work in rib for a further 13 rows.
Row 1 (RS): P18 (18: 21: 21: 24: 24) sts, work across 32 sts of row 1 of sleeve cable pattern, P18 (18: 21: 21: 24: 24) sts.
Row 2: K18 (18: 21: 21: 24: 24) sts, work across 32 sts of row 2 of sleeve cable pattern, K18 (18: 21: 21: 24: 24) sts.

Last 2 rows set sleeve cable pattern with rev st st on either side.
Work in pattern, repeating rows 1 - 12 throughout, AT SAME TIME, inc 1 st at each end every foll 6th (6th: 6th: 4th: 6th: 6th) row to 112 (120: 130: 140: 140: 144) sts, bringing increase sts into rev st st.
Cont without shaping until sleeve measures 52 (53: 54: 55: 56: 57.5) cm, ending with a WS row.
Cast off in pattern.

MAKING UP
Press as described on the information page.
Join both shoulder seams using mattress stitch.

Neckband
Using 3.25mm (US 3) circular needle, pick up and knit 28 sts down left front neck, knit 24 sts from front neck holder, pick up and knit 28 sts up right front neck, knit 34 (38: 38: 42: 42: 46) sts from back neck stitch holder. 114 [118: 118: 122: 122: 126] sts. Join to work in round, placing marker at beg of rnd.
Next Rnd: *K1, P1, rep from * to end.
Rep last rnd 6 times more.
Cast off loosely in pattern.
Place markers 22 (23: 25: 27: 27: 28) cm down from shoulders on front and back. Sew top of sleeve between markers.
Join side and sleeve seams.

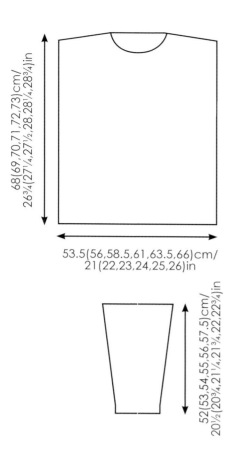

68(69,70,71,72,73)cm/
26³⁄₄(27¹⁄₄,27¹⁄₂,28,28¹⁄₄,28³⁄₄)in

53.5(56,58.5,61,63.5,66)cm/
21(22,23,24,25,26)in

52(53,54,55,56,57.5)cm/
20¹⁄₂(20³⁄₄,21¹⁄₄,21³⁄₄,22,22³⁄₄)in

BEACHMONT

—

SIZE

	S	M	L	XL	XXL	XXXL	cm
To fit chest							
	102	107	112	117	122	127	cm
	40	42	44	46	48	50	in
Actual chest measurement of garment							
	108	112	116	122	128	132	cm
	42½	44	45½	48	50½	52	in

YARN

Rowan Cotton Cashmere

A – Paper 210							
	9	10	11	11	12	13	x 50gm
B – Charcoal 232							
	1	1	1	1	1	1	x 50gm

NEEDLES

4mm (no 8) (US 6) needles
4mm (no 8) (US 6) circular needle, 40 cm / 16 in long

EXTRAS

Stitch holders
Stitch markers

TENSION

20 sts and 28 rows to 10 cm / 4 in measured over st st using 4mm (US 6) needles.

Stripe Sequence

Working in st st throughout, *work 2 rows with yarn B, work 12 rows with yarn A, rep from *.
These 14 rows set stripe sequence.

BACK

Using 4mm (US 6) needles and yarn A, cast on 108 (112: 116: 122: 128: 132) sts.
Next Row (RS): *K1, P1, rep from * to end.
Last row sets rib pattern.
Work in rib pattern for a further 7 rows, ending with a WS row.
Starting with a K row, work in st st as folls:
Begin stripe sequence and cont in st st until back measures 66 (67: 68: 69: 70: 71) cm, ending with a WS row.

Shape shoulders

Cast off 40 (42: 43: 46: 48: 50) sts at beg of next 2 rows. 28 [28: 30: 30: 32: 32] sts.
Leave rem sts on a holder for back neck.

FRONT

Work as for back until 24 rows less have been worked to start of shoulder shaping, ending with a WS row.

Shape front neck

Next Row (RS): K43 (45: 46: 49: 51: 53), turn. Leave rem sts unworked.
Next Row: Purl.
Next Row: K to last 2 sts, K2tog. 42 [44: 45: 48: 50: 52] sts.
Work 3 rows.
Rep last 4 rows twice more. 40 [42: 43: 46: 48: 50] sts.
Cont straight until front is the same length as back to start of shoulder shaping, ending with a WS row.
Cast off.
With RS facing, slip next 22 (22: 24: 24: 26: 26) sts onto a stitch holder. Rejoin yarn to rem 43 (45: 46: 49: 51: 53) sts and knit to end.
Work as for other side of neck, reversing shapings.

SLEEVES

Using 4mm (US 6) needles and yarn A, cast on 48 (50: 50: 56: 60: 60) sts.

Row 1 (RS): * K1, P1, rep from * to end.
Last row sets rib pattern.
Work in rib pattern for a further 7 rows ending with a WS row.
Starting with a K row, work in st st for 4 rows.
Begin stripe sequence and keeping patt correct throughout, inc 1 st at each end of next and every foll 6th row to 84 (92: 100: 108: 108: 112) sts.
Cont without shaping until sleeve measures 52 (54: 57: 59: 60: 62) cm, ending with a WS row.
Cast off.

MAKING UP

Press as described on the information page.
Join both shoulder seams using mattress stitch.

Neckband

Using 4mm (US 6) circular needle and yarn A, pick up and knit 18 sts down left front neck, knit 22 (22: 24: 24: 26: 26) sts from front neck stitch holder, pick up and knit 18 sts up right front neck, knit 28 (28: 30: 30: 32: 32) sts from back neck stitch holder. 86 [86: 90: 90: 94: 94] sts.
Join to work in round, placing marker at beg of rnd.
Next Rnd: * K1, P1, rep from * to end.
Last rnd sets rib pattern.
Work in rib pattern for a further 4 rnds.
Cast off loosely in pattern.
Place markers 21 (23: 25: 27: 27: 28) cm down from shoulders on front and back. Sew top of sleeve between markers.
Join side and sleeve seams.

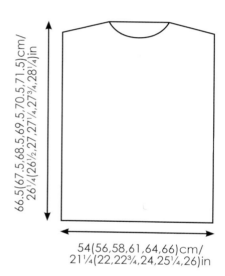

66.5(67.5,68.5,69.5,70.5,71.5)cm/
26¼(26½,27,27¼,27¾,28¼)in

54(56,58,61,64,66)cm/
21¼(22,22¾,24,25¼,26)in

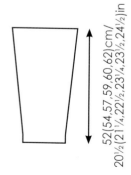

52(54,57,59,60,62)cm/
20½(21¼,22½,23¼,23½,24½)in

FAIRDALE

—

SIZE

	S	M	L	XL	XXL	XXXL	cm
To fit chest							
	102	107	112	117	122	127	cm
	40	42	44	46	48	50	in
Actual chest measurement of garment							
	113	118	123.5	128	133.5	136	cm
	44½	46½	48½	50½	52½	53½	in

YARN

Rowan Moordale

6	6	7	7	8	9	x 100gm

(photographed in Thai 05)

NEEDLES

4mm (no 8) (US 6) needles
4mm (no 8) (US 6) circular needle, 40 cm / 16 in long

EXTRAS

Stitch holders
Stitch markers

TENSION

24 sts and 28 rows to 10 cm / 4 in measured over rib
using 4mm (US 6) needles **once blocked.**

BACK

Using 4mm (US 6) needles, cast on 134 (140: 146: 152:
158: 162) sts.
Next Row (RS): K2 (0: 2: 0: 2: 2), * P2, K2 rep
from * to end.
Next Row: *P2, K2 rep from * to last 2 (0: 2: 0: 2: 2) sts,
P2 (0: 2: 0: 2: 2).
Last 2 rows set rib pattern.
Work in rib pattern for a further 10 rows, increasing
1 st at each end on last row. 136 [142: 148: 154:
160: 164] sts.
Next Row (RS): *K1, P1, rep from * to end.
Last row sets single rib pattern.
Cont in single rib patt as folls:

Optional lower back short rows (to add length to back of sweater)

Work in single rib patt until back measures
approximately 15 cm / 6 in, ending with a WS row.
Keeping single rib patt correct, work short rows as folls:
Row 1 (RS): Work in rib to last 5 sts, wrap and turn.

Row 2: Work in rib to last 5 sts, wrap and turn.
Row 3 (RS): Work in rib to last 8 sts, wrap and turn.
Row 4: Work in rib to last 8 sts, wrap and turn.
Row 5 (RS): Work in rib to last 10 sts, wrap and turn.
Row 6: Work in rib to last 10 sts, wrap and turn.
Next row (RS): Work in rib to end of row, picking up
loops from wrap stitches.
Cont in single rib patt until back measures 65 (66: 67:
68: 69: 69) cm, ending with a WS row.

Shape shoulders

Cast off 23 (24: 25: 26: 27: 28) sts at beg of next 4 rows.
44 [46: 48: 50: 52: 52] sts.
Leave rem sts on a stitch holder for back neck.

FRONT

Work as for back (omitting optional lower back short
rows) until 46 (48: 50: 52: 54: 54) rows less have been
worked to start of shoulder shaping, ending with a
WS row.

Shape front neck

Next Row (RS): Patt 68 (71: 74: 77: 80: 82) sts, turn.
Leave rem sts unworked.
Next row (WS): Patt to end.
Cont working in patt, decreasing 1 st at neck edge
on next and every alt row until 46 (48: 50: 52: 54: 56) sts
remain, ending with a WS row.

Shape shoulders

Cast off 23 (24: 25: 26: 27: 28) sts at beg of next and foll alt row.
Fasten off.
With RS facing, rejoin yarn to rem 68 (71: 74: 77: 80: 82) sts and patt to end.
Work as for other side of neck, reversing shapings.

SLEEVES

Using 4mm (US 6) needles, cast on 62 sts.
Row 1 (RS): K2, *P2, K2, rep from * to end.
Row 2: *P2, K2, rep from * to last 2 sts, P2.
Last 2 rows set rib pattern.
Work in rib pattern for a further 10 rows.
Next Row: * K1, P1, rep from * to end.
Last row sets single rib pattern.
Working in single rib patt throughout, inc 1 st at each end of every foll 4th row to 120 (124: 124: 128: 128: 128) sts, bringing increase sts into single rib patt.
Cont without shaping until sleeve measures 52 (54: 56: 58: 60: 62) cm, ending with a WS row.
Cast off loosely in pattern.

MAKING UP

Press as described on the information page.
Join both shoulder seams using mattress stitch.

Crossover V-neck Neckband

Using 4mm (US 6) circular needle and starting at front centre point, pick up and knit 41 (44: 45: 48: 49: 51) sts up right front neck, knit 44 (46: 48: 50: 52: 52) sts from back neck stitch holder, pick up and knit 41 (44: 45: 48: 49: 51) sts down left front neck. 126 [134: 138: 146: 150: 154] sts. Do not join, work back and forth in rows.
Next Row (WS): *P2, K2 rep from * to last 2 sts, P2.
Nest Row: K2, *P2, K2, rep from * to end.
Last 2 rows set rib pattern.
Work in rib pattern for a further 10 rows.
Cast off loosely in pattern.
Join left side of neckband to pick up seam of right side of neck, join right side of neck to left front seam.
Place markers 25 (26: 26: 27: 27: 27) cm down from shoulders on front and back. Sew top of sleeve between markers.
Join side and sleeve seams.

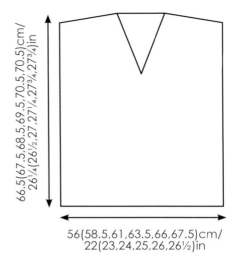

66.5(67.5,68.5,69.5,70.5,70.5)cm/
26¼(26½,27,27¼,27¾,27¾)in

56(58.5,61,63.5,66,67.5)cm/
22(23,24,25,26,26½)in

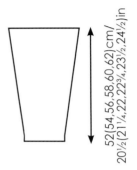

52(54,56,58,60,62)cm/
20½(21¼,22,22¾,23½,24½)in

CARBON

—

SIZE
To fit an average-size adult man's head

YARN
Felted Tweed Aran
    3 x 50gm
(photographed in Carbon 759)

NEEDLES
5mm (US 8) circular needle, 40 cm / 16 in long
Set of four 5mm (US 8) double-pointed needles (dpn's)

EXTRAS
3 stitch markers, + 1 in contrasting colour for beginning of round

TENSION
16 sts and 22 rnds to 10 cm / 4 in measured over st st using 5mm (US 8) needle

HAT
Using 5mm (US 8) circular needle, cast on 96 sts. Join to work in rnd, taking care not to twist sts, and place contrasting marker (pm) for beg of rnd.
Rnd 1: *K2, P2, rep from * to end.
This round forms double rib.
Repeat last rnd until work measures 28 cm / 11 in.
Place markers after the 29th st, 61st st and 93rd st.

Shape crown
Changing to dpn's when necessary, work as folls:
Rnd 1: *Work in double rib until two sts before marker, K2tog, sl marker, SSK, rep from * to end. 90 sts.
Rnd 2: Rep rnd 1. 84 sts.
Rnd 3: Work in double rib to end.
Rep rnds 1–3 five times more. 24 sts.
Rnd 19: *Work in double rib until two sts before marker, K2tog, sl marker, SSK, rep from * to end. 18 sts.
Rnd 20: *Work in double rib until two sts before marker, K2tog, sl marker, SSK, rep from * to end. 12 sts.

MAKING UP
Break yarn and thread through rem sts, pull up tight and fasten off securely.
Press as described on the information page.

RIVET

SIZE
Width: 20 cm / 8 in
Length: 149 cm / 58 ¾ in

YARN
Rowan Island Blend
A - Jet 902
     3 x 50gm
B - Marine 905
     3 x 50gm
C - Ash 901
     1 x 50gm

NEEDLES
4mm (US 6) circular needle, 40 cm / 16 in long
Set of four 5mm (US 8) double-pointed needles (dpn's)

EXTRAS
Stitch marker

TENSION
21 sts and 28 rnds to 10 cm / 4 in measured over st st
using 4mm (US 6) needle

SCARF
Using 4mm (US 6) needle and yarn A, cast on 88 sts.
Join to work in rnd, taking care not to twist sts, and
place marker (pm) for beg of rnd.
Rnd 1: K to end.
This rnd forms st st.
Rnds 2-28: Cont with yarn A in st st.
Break yarn A and join yarn B.
Rnds 29-56: With yarn B, work in st st for 28 rnds.
Break yarn B and join yarn A.
Rnds 57-84: With yarn A, work in st st for 28 rnds.
Break yarn A and join yarn C.
Rnds 85-87: With yarn C, work in st st for 3 rnds.
Rnds 88-90: With yarn A, work in st st for 3 rnds.
Rnds 91-108: Rep rnds 85-90 three times more.
Rnds 109-111: Rep rnds 85-87 once more.
Repeat Rnds 1-111 for stripe pattern twice more,
then Rnds 1-84 once more.
Next rnd: With yarn A, K.

MAKING UP
Leaving sts live, divide sts onto two dpn's (first 44 sts on
needle 1 and last 44 sts on needle 2) and using third
dpn, work a three-needle bind off using yarn A. Pick
up and divide cast-on sts onto two dpn's (first 44 sts on
needle 1 and last 44 sts on needle 2). Using third dpn,
work a three-needle bind off using yarn A.
Press as described on the information page.

CAMERON

—

SIZE
Width: 27.5 cm / 10¾ in
Length: 228 cm / 90 in

YARN
Felted Tweed Aran
A - Carbon 759
        5 x 50gm
B - Granite 719
        5 x 50gm
C - Sea Storm 784
        5 x 50gm

NEEDLES
5mm (US 8) circular needle, 40 cm / 16 in long
Set of four 5mm (US 8) double-pointed needles (dpn's)

EXTRAS
Stitch marker

TENSION
16 sts and 23 rnds to 10cm / 4 in measured over st st
using 5mm (US 8) needle

SCARF
Using 5mm (US 8) needle and yarn A, cast on 88 sts.
Join to work in rnd, taking care not to twist sts, and
place marker (pm) for beg of rnd.
Rnd 1: K to end.
This rnd forms st st.
Cont with yarn A in st st until work measures 76 cm / 30 in.
Break yarn A and join yarn B.

With yarn B, cont in st st until work measures
152 cm / 60 in.
Break yarn B and join yarn C.

With yarn C, cont in st st until work measures
228 cm / 90 in.

MAKING UP
Leaving sts live, divide sts onto two dpn's (first 44 sts on
needle 1 and last 44 sts on needle 2) and using third
dpn, work a three-needle bind off using yarn C.
Pick up and divide cast-on sts onto two dpn's (first 44 sts
on needle 1 and last 44 sts on needle 2). Using third
dpn, work a three-needle bind off using yarn A.
Press as described on the information page.

BEDFORD

—

SIZE
To fit an average-size adult man's head

YARN
Rowan Island Blend
A - Leather 903
     2 x 50gm
B - Jet 902
     1 x 50gm

NEEDLES
4mm (US 6) circular needle 40 cm /16 in long
Set of four 4mm (US 6) double-pointed needles (dpn's)

EXTRAS
Stitch marker

TENSION
21 sts and 28 rnds to 10 cm / 4 in measured over st st
using 4mm (US 6) needle

HAT
Using 4mm (US 6) needle and yarn B, cast on 120 sts.
Join to work in rnd, taking care not to twist sts, and
place marker (pm) for beg of rnd.
Rnd 1: *K1, P1, rep from * to end.
This round forms single rib.
Repeat last rnd 3 times more.
Break yarn B and join yarn A.
Next Rnd: With yarn A, cont in single rib until work
measures 15 cm / 6 in.
This round forms st st.
Cont in st st for 5 cm / 2 in.

Shape crown
Changing to dpn's when necessary, work as folls:
Rnd 1: *K10, K2tog, rep from * to end. 110 sts.
Next and all alt rnds: K to end.
Rnd 3: *K9, K2tog, rep from * to end. 100 sts.
Rnd 5: *K8, K2tog, rep from * to end. 90 sts.
Rnd 7: *K7, K2tog, rep from * to end. 80 sts.
Rnd 9: *K6, K2tog, rep from * to end. 70 sts.

Rnd 11: *K5, K2tog, rep from * to end. 60 sts.
Rnd 13: *K4, K2tog, rep from * to end. 50 sts.
Rnd 15: *K3, K2tog, rep from * to end. 40 sts.
Rnd 17: *K2, K2tog, rep from * to end. 30 sts.
Rnd 19: *K1, K2tog, rep from * to end. 20 sts
Rnd 21: *K2tog, rep from * to end. 10 sts.

MAKING UP
Break yarn and thread through rem sts, pull up tight
and fasten off securely.
Press as described on the information page.

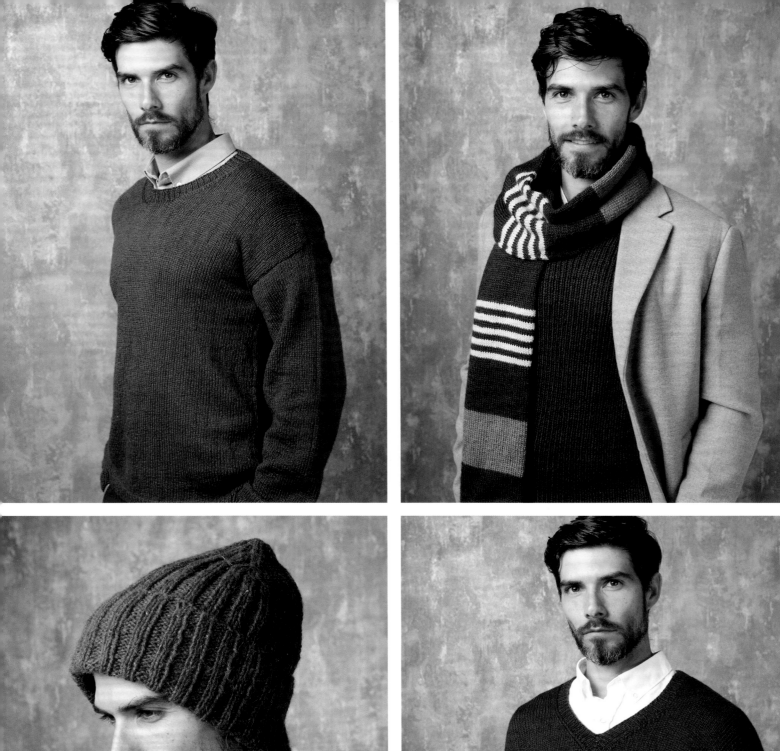

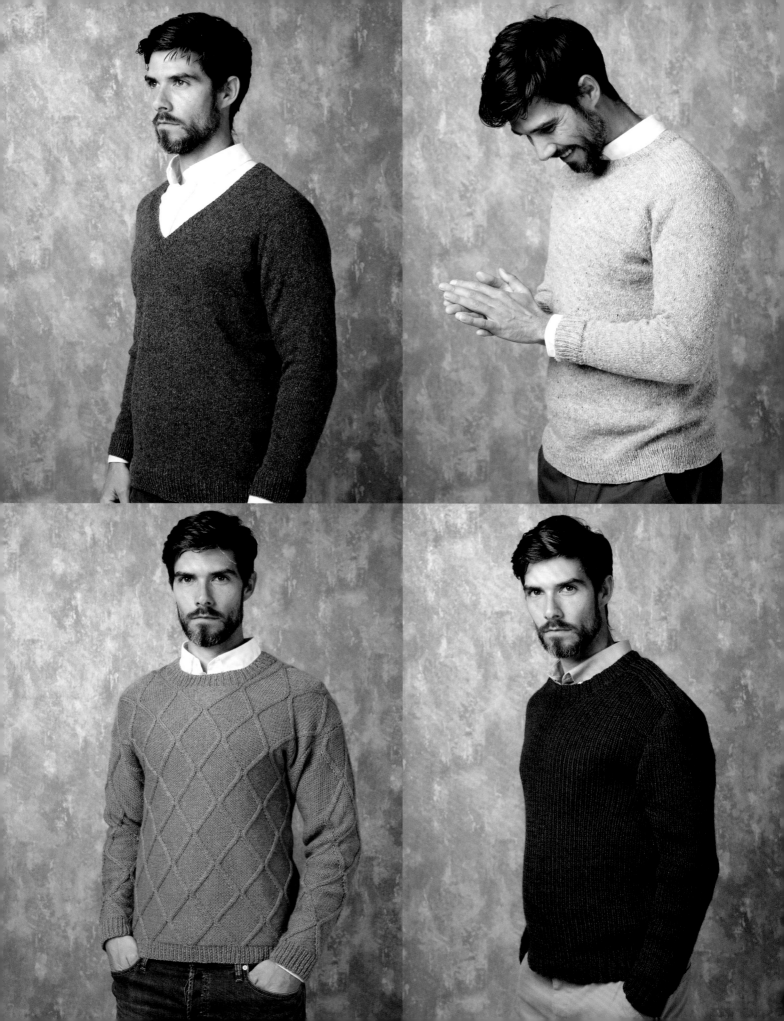

INFORMATION
—

TENSION

Obtaining the correct tension is perhaps the single factor which can make the difference between a successful garment and a disastrous one. It controls both the shape and size of an article, so any variation, however slight, can distort the finished garment. Different designers feature in our books and it is their tension, given at the start of each pattern, which you must match. We recommend that you knit a square in pattern and/or stocking stitch (depending on the pattern instructions) of perhaps 5 - 10 more stitches and 5 - 10 more rows than those given in the tension note. Mark out the central 10cm square with pins. If you have too many stitches to 10cm try again using thicker needles, if you have too few stitches to 10cm try again using finer needles. Once you have achieved the correct tension your garment will be knitted to the measurements indicated in the size diagram shown at the end of the pattern.

After working for hours knitting a garment, it seems a great pity that many garments are spoiled because such little care is taken in the pressing and finishing process. Follow the text below for a truly professional-looking garment.

Block out each piece of knitting and following the instructions on the ball band press the garment pieces, omitting the ribs. Tip: Take special care to press the edges, as this will make sewing up both easier and neater. If the ball band indicates that the fabric is not to be pressed, then covering the blocked out fabric with a damp white cotton cloth and leaving it to stand will have the desired effect. Darn in all ends neatly along the selvage edge or a colour join, as appropriate.

STITCHING

When stitching the pieces together, remember to match areas of colour and texture very carefully where they meet. Use a seam stitch such as back stitch or mattress stitch for all main knitting seams and join all ribs and neckband with mattress stitch, unless otherwise stated.

CONSTRUCTION

Having completed the pattern instructions, join left shoulder and neckband seams as detailed above. Sew the top of the sleeve to the body of the garment using the method detailed in the pattern, referring to the appropriate guide:
Straight cast-off sleeves: Place centre of cast-off edge of sleeve to shoulder seam.

Sew top of sleeve to body, using markers as guidelines where applicable.

Square set-in sleeves: Place centre of cast-off edge of sleeve to shoulder seam. Set sleeve head into armhole, the straight sides at top of sleeve to form a neat right-angle to cast-off sts at armhole on back and front.

Shallow set-in sleeves: Place centre of cast off edge of sleeve to shoulder seam. Match decreases at beg of armhole shaping to decreases at top of sleeve. Sew sleeve head into armhole, easing in shapings.

Set-in sleeves: Place centre of cast-off edge of sleeve to shoulder seam. Set in sleeve, easing sleeve head into armhole. Join side and sleeve seams.
Slip stitch pocket edgings and linings into place.
Sew on buttons to correspond with buttonholes.
Ribbed welts and neckbands and any areas of garter stitch should not be pressed.

ABBREVIATIONS

K	knit
P	purl
st(s)	stitch(es)
inc	increas(e)(ing)
dec	decreas(e)(ing)
st st	stocking stitch (1 row K, 1 row P)
g st	garter stitch (K every row)
beg	begin(ning)
foll	following
rem	remain(ing)
rev st st	reverse stocking stitch (1 row K , 1 row P)
rep	repeat
alt	alternate
cont	continue
patt	pattern
tog	together
mm	millimetres
cm	centimetres
in(s)	inch(es)
RS	right side
WS	wrong side
sl 1	slip one stitch
psso	pass slipped stitch over
p2sso	pass 2 slipped stitches over
tbl	through back of loop
M1	make one stitch by picking up horizontal loop before next stitch and knitting into back of it
M1P	make one stitch by picking up horizontal loop before next stitch and purlinginto back of it
yfwd	yarn forward
yrn	yarn round needle
meas	measures
0	no stitches, times or rows
-	no stitches, times or rows for that size
yo	yarn over needle
yfrn	yarn forward round needle
wyib	with yarn at back
sl2togK	slip 2 stitches together knitways

MACHINE WASH SYMBOLS

HAND WASH SYMBOLS

DRY CLEAN SYMBOLS

IRONING SYMBOLS

DO NOT BLEACH SYMBOL

DRYING SYMBOLS

MODEL SIZE INFORMATION

Model wears UK size S / 40 in chest

STANDARD MENS AND UNISEX SIZING GUIDE

Mens sizes: S to XXXL. Unisex Sizes: S to XXXL

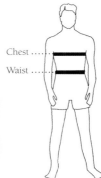

Chest ......
Waist ......

UK SIZE	S	M	L	XL	XXL	XXXL	
To fit chest	40	42	44	46	48	50	inches
	102	107	112	117	122	127	cm
To fit waist	32	34	36	38	40	42	inches
	81	86	91	97	102	107	cm

MEASUREMENT WORKSHEET

Using a tape measure, take the following measurements (of yourself or the individual you are knitting for) and record them here, keeping this worksheet handy for future reference. For accuracy, take measurements while you or the person you are knitting for is wearing the same undergarments or undershirt your or they would typically wear under a sweater.

MEASUREMENTS

Chest:

Length (centre back of neck to bottom edge):

Upper arm circumference:

Length of underarm to bottom of sleeve:

Neck:

Waist:

Wrist:

Notes:

You can also measure a favourite sweater. This will ensure the size you choose will fit well. If you need to adjust the sleeve length, or knit the torso a bit longer than written in the pattern, you can plan for those adjustments before you begin knitting.

FAVOURITE SWEATER from closet

Chest:

Length (centre back of neck to bottom edge):

Upper arm circumference:

Length of underarm to bottom of sleeve:

Neck:

Waist:

Wrist: